HANDWRITING Notebook

This book belongs to

Made in the USA
Monee, IL
10 September 2024

65424367R00057